BOOK ANALYSIS

Written by Sophie Urbain
Translated by Emma Lunt

AF126344

Moby-Dick,
or The Whale

BY HERMAN MELVILLE

Bright
≡Summaries.com

HERMAN MELVILLE

ADVENTURE WRITER

- **Born in New York in 1819**
- **Died there in 1891**
- **Notable works:**
  - *Pierre; or, The Ambiguities* (1852), novel
  - *Benito Cereno* (1855), novel
  - *Bartleby, the Scrivener* (1856), novel
  - *Billy Budd* (1891, published posthumously in 1924), novel

Melville was born to a middle-class family of traders in New York. He had a difficult childhood, during which he had to deal with the death of his father when he was 13 years old. In 1841, he joined a whaling crew and left after 18 months of sailing, during a stopover on the Marquesas Islands, where he lived for many months with a cannibal tribe. He managed to escape and sailed on different whalers before boarding an American military ship which brought him to Boston in 1844.

His sea adventures inspired his novels, such as *Typee* (1846), which recounts his stay on the Marquesas Islands. *Moby-Dick; or, The Whale* (sometimes known simply as *Moby Dick*) was published in 1851, but was a complete failure, just like *Pierre; or, The Ambiguities* (1852). The same happened with his short stories, *Bartleby* (1856) and *Benito Cereno* (1855), which saw no success. In order to support himself financially, Melville was forced to accept a position as a customs officer in New York. He died in 1891 in destitution and anonymity.

MOBY-DICK, OR THE WHALE

A SYMBOLIC ODYSSEY

- **Genre:** novel
- **Reference edition:** Melville, H. (1983) *Moby-Dick, or The Whale*. California: University of California Press.
- **First edition:** 1851
- **Themes:** the sea, hunting, whales, faith, pride, vengeance, man's fight against evil

Moby-Dick, or, The Whale is an almost undefinable novel due to the fact that it explores various genres. It tells the story of Ishmael, a young sailor that wishes to return to the sea and decides to board a whaler. With his companion Queequeg, they join the *Pequod*, a ship belonging to the terrible Captain Ahab. At sea, the captain and his crew hunt whales, to collect their precious oil which they will then sell at port. But Ahab is actually pursuing a different goal: to find Moby Dick, the monstrous white whale that tore off his leg, and to get revenge on him.

Published in 1851, both the public and critics were generally unaware of *Moby-Dick; or, The Whale*. It was only recognised as one of the most important novels in American literature many years after the author's death. Nevertheless, its late success led to it being the subject of numerous adaptations, from cinema and television, to theatre and literature.

SUMMARY

PART ONE – A THIRST FOR THE OCEAN

Ishmael, the story's narrator, is a young sailor who wants to board a ship to go and hunt whales. During his research, he discovers New Bedford and Nantucket, two renowned whaling ports in the United States at the time, as well as the whole atmosphere of big fishing ports: foggy docks, singing hostels and filled with sailors waiting to depart.

In the hostel where he has chosen to stay before embarking, Ishmael meets Queequeg, a native of the southern isles and a harpooner, covered in scars all over his body and always carrying a human head and a wooden idol with him. Together, the two men join the *Pequod*, the ship belonging to the ship-owners Bildad and Peleg, retired, veteran sailors and commanded by the mysterious Captain Ahab. Before leaving, they meet a mysterious person named Elijah, according to prophecy, who begs them not to board this unlucky ship. The *Pequod* does indeed have a worrying appearance, decorated all over with the remains of its enemies; ivory bones and whalebone plates (corneal strips hang from the cetacean palace) decorate the ship, while the captain's false leg is cut from a toothed whale's jawbone.

PART TWO – A MYSTERIOUS CAPTAIN

The whole crew knows the story of Captain Ahab: during his previous voyage, he had encountered a monstrous white whale, followed it into the sea and lost his leg during a fight with the animal. This white monster is well known by all the whalers: he is known as Moby Dick. It is then in the second part that the reader is faced with cetology, the science of cetaceans.

For lack of being able to describe the captain, who is always invisible to the crew, Ishmael gives the reader information about the other crew members, whom he compares with knights and squires. There are officers, who are all American, whalemen and also chief mates – Starbuck, Stubb and Flask – and their hopeful harpooners, the foreigners – Queequeg, Tashtego and Daggoo. The rest of the crew is also made up of men of foreign origin. It is only in chapter 28 that Captain Ahab appears, giving Ishmael the chance to describe him.

PART THREE – HUNTING THE WHALE

After some weeks of sailing, Captain Ahab holds a meeting at the back of the ship and exposes his true intentions: they have not embarked on a hunt for any whale to sell, they are actually tracking Moby Dick, so that Ahab can get his revenge. The captain, through an inspiring speech and some financial incentive – an ounce of gold for the first person to spot the whale -, manages to convince the men to follow him in his journey, despite the reluctance of his chief mate, Starbuck: "I came here to hunt whales, not my commander's vengeance. How many barrels of thy vengeance yield thee even if thou gettest it, Captain Ahab?" (Chapter 36).

The *Pequod* encounters many other ships (The *Albatross,* the *Tow-Ho,* the *Jeroboam,* the *Virgin,* the *Rose-Bud,* the *Samuel Enderby,* the *Bachelor,* the *Rachel,* the *Delight*), who Ahab asks for information about the white whale: if it has been seen recently and, if so, when and where.

While waiting to find Moby Dick, the *Pequod* sails around and hunts the whales that they meet along their route. The descriptions of the hunt alternate between taking on a lyrical and a realistic tone with tangents about the anatomy and principles of the whales, and about the techniques used to hunt and to carve up the whales. The narrator also explains how the whale's different body parts are used: its fat serves to make oil for candles; its flesh is eaten by the sailors; its spermaceti organ (situated in the head) is collected to make high quality candles; its bones and non-usable parts are used as fuel in the ship's boilers. All of these digressions are not completely useless to the story: they create a mythology about the whale, and Moby Dick in particular, arousing the reader's desire to see him emerge from the surface of the water so that Ahab can finally accomplish his goal.

PART FOUR – AHAB'S FINAL HUNT

Having discovered traces of the white whale, the *Pequod* follows him for three days. The hunt ends in hand-to-hand combat when Moby Dick, opening his gaping mouth, grabs Ahab's rowing boat, who takes hold of his immense jaw to make him let go. Moby Dick is the winner: many of the small boats are broken on the first day and the sailors return to the ship before nightfall.

On the second day, Moby Dick uses the same tactic: he destroys several rowing boats and throws himself on Ahab's, whose ivory leg is shattered in the fray. The *Pequod* collects its shipwrecked sailors, and the ship's carpenter gets to work repairing the captain's broken leg. The sailors also notice that Fedallah, Ahab's harpooner, has disappeared. On the third day, not seeing the whale, Ahab thinks that they have passed it in the night and orders them to turn around. Starbuck, the chief mate, is convinced that victory is not possible against this monster and that continuing this hunt is an offence against God. Ahab still orders them to take to the water in their rowing boats and everybody searches for Moby Dick on the calm sea waters.

Suddenly, he reappears, bursting from the depths, and with one blow of his tail, separates the fleet of small boats, shattering those belonging to the two chief mates and leaving Ahab's intact. When he re-enters the fray, the sailors discover, to their horror, Fedallah's body which has been torn to shreds, tangled in the lines and harpoons driven into the monster's body the day before. Ahab is more determined than ever. Getting to the side of the whale, he launches his harpoon. Moby Dick rolls to the side and tips over Ahab's boat. As he is about to launch himself on the rowing boat to break it, the line breaks and Moby Dick changes direction, throwing himself right onto the *Pequod*, which is watching the scene from a distance. Ahab rushes to get back to the ship, but the front of his boat, which has been damaged by Moby Dick, breaks, allowing water in. The crew that have stayed on the ship see Moby Dick coming who, like the wave of the Last Judgement, breaks the front of the *Pequod*. Enraged by the loss of his ship, Ahab relaunches his harpoon but the line tangles and Moby Dick pounces on the captain, pulling him under. The whole crew perishes, followed by the ship which sinks in the water.

Only Ishmael, clinging to a piece of the wreckage, witnesses the entire scene and survives it. Floating on a piece of his boat, he is pulled out of the water by the *Rachel*, the ship that is looking for the men it has lost at sea: "In her retracing search after her missing children, only found another orphan" (Epilogue). Only one life has been saved, one witness to the story, like this phrase extracted from the Book of Job (one of the books of the Old Testament) at the start of the epilogue: "And I only am escaped alone to tell thee" (Epilogue).

CHARACTER STUDY

MAIN CHARACTERS

Ishmael

Attracted to the sea and open water, Ishmael wants to board a boat to hunt whales:

> "Chief among these motives was the overwhelming idea of the great whale himself. Such a portentous and mysterious monster roused all my curiosity. Then the wild and distant seas where he rolled his island bulk; the undeliverable, nameless perils of the whale; these, with all the attending marvels of a thousand Patagonian sights and sounds, helped to sway me to my wish. [...] I am tormented with an everlasting itch for things remote. I love to sail forbidden seas, and land on barbarous coasts." (Chapter 1).

His name, a biblical reference, also defines his character: he is a recluse, a non-conformist, an exile who feels alienated by human society and flees from it. In the Bible, Ishmael is the son of Abraham. The latter's wife, Sarah, is unable to give him a descendent, which therefore pushes her servant, Agar, into the arms of her husband. Ishmael is a product of this relationship. But, later, Sarah finally succeeds in giving Abraham a son, Isaac. In order for this son to be Abraham's only inheritor, Sarah forces Agar and her son Ishmael to go into exile in the desert.

This marginality also appears in his choice of accommodation at the start of the novel: he chooses a calm, even deserted, hostel when he has passed many other establishments that are much louder and livelier. Ishmael's isolation is also noticeable in his rejection of human contact, notably when the hostel owner tells him that he is going to have to share his bed with somebody. At first, he refuses and chooses to sleep on a bench in the hostel's common room. Later, on the ship, Ishmael doesn't form any particular bonds with the other crew members – except with Queequeg, his roommate; he is happy just to be there, on board.

He witnesses the story, but does not seem to – or does not want to – take part in it. He watches the activities on board the *Pequod*, but the action seems to take place in front of his eyes without him really participating in it. He gives the impression of being an observer stationed on the ship to describe what happens.

Ahab

With a large and tall build, he is a robust man with grey hair. A pale white scar begins at his hairline and stretches the length of his face and neck to disappear under his clothes. Nobody knows whether this is a birth mark or the mark of a past injury. Having lost his leg in a previous fight with Moby Dick, he wears a prosthetic made of ivory from the jawbone of a toothed whale. The tapping of this leg on the ship's deck wakes the sailors every night. His relentlessness and obsession with hunting Moby Dick at any cost drives him to stay pent-up in his cabin, studying his maritime maps and searching in vain for where this white monster could be hiding:

"Almost every night some pencil marks where effaced, and others were substituted. For with the charts of all four oceans behind him, Ahab was threading a maze of currents and eddies, with a view to the more certain accomplishment of that monomaniac though of his soul. [...] [Ahab] knew the sets of all tides and currents; and thereby calculating the driftings of the sperm whale's food; and, also, calling to mind the regular, ascertained season for hunting him in particular latitude; could arrive at reasonable surmises, almost approaching to certainties, concerning the timeliest day to be upon this or that ground in search of his prey" (Chapter 44).

Ahab also shows his secrecy regarding the sailors, who he does not tell about the true goal of the voyage. His plan is only revealed in Chapter 36, when the *Pequod* cast off in Chapter 22. Furthermore, Ahab promises a reward of gold (a doubloon) to whoever points out the white whale first. By doing this, he brings the soldiers' personal interest into play and not just the common interest of everybody. In fact, each crew member receives a part of the earnings from fishing, according to the skill demonstrated and the work produced on board. Ahab therefore turns a trade business around in favour of personal vengeance.

Through good scheming and without losing sight of his ultimate goal, the old captain continues an ordinary whale hunt for some time, as along the path they must follow to Moby Dick, the sailors put their whalers into the water to kill some cetaceans several times.

Moby Dick

A white, monstrous toothed whale, Moby Dick is gifted in mischief:

> "It was not so much his uncommon bulk that so much distinguished him from other sperm whales, but, as was elsewhere thrown out – a peculiar snow-white wrinkled forehead, and a high, pyramidical white hump. [...]. The rest of his body was so streaked, and spotted, and marbled with the same shrouded hue, that, in the end, he had gained his distinctive appellation of the White Whale [...]. Nor was it his unwonted magnitude, nor his remarkable hue, nor yet his deformed lower jaw, that so much invested the whale with natural terror, as that unexampled, intelligent malignity which, according to specific accounts, he had over and over again evinced in his assaults. More than all, his treacherous retreats struck more of dismay than perhaps aught else. [...] such seemed the White Whale's infernal aforethought of ferocity, that every dismembering or death that he caused, was not wholly regarded as having been inflicted by an unintelligent agent." (Chapter 41).

He is, for the sailors and above all for Ahab, the personification of evil: "The White Whale swam before him as the monomaniac incarnation of all those malicious agencies which some deep men feel eating in them, till they are left living on with half a heart and half a lung" (Chapter 41). Having had his leg torn off by this monster during his last whaling trip, Ahab has hunted him relentlessly through the oceans to exact his revenge, but the whale turns out to be more powerful.

THE OFFICERS AND HARPOONERS

Starbuck

Originating from Nantucket, Starbuck, the first chief mate of the *Pequod*, is a tall, thin and serious man, his face and body marked by his many travels. His skin is so tanned by the warm draughts that it resembles tempered biscuit dough and he seems: "prepared to endure for long ages to come, and to endure always, as now; for be it Polar snow of torrid sun" (Chapter 26). Starbuck is the only one to dare to stand up to Captain Ahab. Meticulous in his role as a sailor, he shows clever superstition, and his predictions and premonitions often turn out to be true.

Stubb

Originating from Cape Cod, Stubb, the second chief mate on the *Pequod*, is a nonchalant man, neither cowardly nor brave. He shows a sort of indifference towards life events and takes danger as it comes. "So cheerily trudging off with the burden of life" (Chapter 27). Always even-tempered, he never goes anywhere without his pipe, which is an integral part of his appearance.

Flask

Originating from Tisbury, Flask is the third chief mate on the *Pequod.* He is a red-headed, short and strong man. Not showing any fear regarding the whales or the danger that hunting them entails, he hates them and loves to hunt them, demonstrating such an aggressive rage that we could say that each whale that he kills had personally offended him.

Queequeg

Originating from the Southern Pacific islands, Queequeg is a tall man whose body is covered with tattoos. He meets Ishmael at the hostel, *The Spouter Inn*, when the latter is forced to share his bed due to a lack of space. One night, they become friends after smoking a pipe together. As is the norm in his country, Queequeg declares that they are henceforth "married", meaning that they each must die for the other if it is necessary.

Ishmael dedicates an entire chapter to telling his story. Although he is described as a pagan, Queequeg observes Ramadan at the start of the novel. On board the *Pequod*, he is Starbuck's harpooner.

Tashtego

Tashtego, Stubb's harpooner, is an Indian originating from Gayhead, with long hair and dark eyes. His harpooning ability is inherited from his bow hunting ancestors in the continent's forests.

Daggoo

Daggoo is described by Ishmael as "a gigantic, coal-black negro-savage, with a lion-like tread" (Chapter 27). He wears big gold earrings and enrolled to be a whale hunter as a child. His large size contrasts with the smallness of Flask, for whom he is the harpooner.

Fedallah

Fedallah, who is of Persian origin and described as "the white-turbaned old man" (Chapter 48), is Captain Ahab's harpooner. His presence on board is not mentioned at the beginning of the book; he only appears at the time of the whale hunt, in Chapter 50. He is not well-liked by Stubb and Flask, who see him as the "the devil in disguise" (Chapter 73).

ANALYSIS

POLYPHONIC NARRATION

Melville's novel is polyphonic in the etymological sense of the word: it actually includes 'many voices'. Not only the voices of different narrators, but the one voice of the narrator using different nuances: the tone of the narration changes according to circumstances. Sometimes, the reader finds themselves faced with the serious and moralistic tone of a priest in his pulpit, sometimes they encounter the gruff style of the sailors, nevertheless capable of some lyrical musings, such as when Ishmael describes the landscape and the sensations of sailing:

> "The vast swells of the omnipotent sea; the surging, hollow roar they made, as they rolled along the eight gunwales, like gigantic bowls in a boundless bowling-green; the brief suspended agony of the boat, as it would tip for an instant on the knife-like edge of the sharper waves, that almost seemed threatening to cut it in two; the sudden profound dip into the watery glens and hollows; the keen spurrings and goadings to gain the top of the opposite hill; the headlong, sled-like slide down its other side;—all these, with the cries of the headsmen and harpooneers, and the shuddering gasps of the oarsmen, with the wondrous sight of the ivory Pequod bearing down upon her boats with outstretched sails, like a wild hen after her screaming brood;—all this was thrilling" (Chapter 48).

The tone is sometimes philosophical. The narrator, Ismael, seems to waste time in another sort of dreaming, an internal monologue through which he reflects on his condition, on the journey and on the goal they are hunting, as is the case at the start of Chapter 49. Humour and irony are also present on the ship, such as when Ishmael, having been pulled out of the water, stops Stubb before he continues with his will:

> Mr. Stubb, I think I have heard you say that of all whalemen you ever met, our chief mate, Mr. Starbuck, is by far the most careful and prudent. I suppose then, that going plump on a flying whale with your sail set in a foggy squall is the height of a whaleman's discretion? (Chapter 49).

Finally, poetry and romanticism are not ignored by Melville, and he features them in the descriptions of the maritime landscapes.

RELIGIOUS SYMBOLISM

Melville's novel is symbolic in many ways. On the one hand, through his many references to the Bible: indeed, what do we say about the characters' names, inspired by some protagonists from the story of the Old Testament? We have Ishmael, Abraham's illegitimate child and, because of this, rejected by everybody and exiled; Ahab, the damned King of Israel, ungodly because he married Jezebel and built her a temple to the god Baal; or even Elijah the prophet, whose sad warning Ishmael does not understand at the start of the novel.

On the other hand, faith holds an importance place in the sailors' lives. In fact, at the start of the novel, Ishmael and

Queequeg visit a chapel, where the families of sailors lost at sea come to gather their thoughts and where the priest's pulpit resembles a ship's bow. In his sermon, this priest tells them the story of Jonah, a prophet that was swallowed by an enormous fish because he did not fulfil the mission that God had given to him. Faith is therefore important onshore, for the sailors' families and loved ones, who wait to see them return safe and sound, praying that they will be saved from the misfortunes of the sea. But it is also important on the sea, because it gives the sailors something to hold onto when everything seems lost. This belief in a divine unity, this higher power that controls the world, choosing the joys and pains of each person, this unshakeable faith that comforts them when, upon seeing Moby Dick, they all board their little boats, having decided to accomplish their captain's vengeance.

We also see many religious denominations in the story: Christianity is of course present, but so is Paganism (the name given to Christians with polytheistic beliefs) in the crew of foreign sailors in the *Pequod*'s crew, and Quakerism (a religious branch derived from Protestantism, based on personal practice of faith) through the officers and Captain Ahab. All of these branches of religious thought cross over on board the ship, but are all in accordance with the idea that one universal God presides over the destiny of each person.

A MAIDEN VOYAGE

Melville's novel is also the story of Ishmael's maiden voyage.

For him, it is about boarding a ship to hunt a whale.

During his journey, the hero looks to cling onto a comforting figure, a sort of father or experienced guide who will accompany him on the journey he is undertaking. In *Moby Dick; or, The Whale*, this role is filled by Queequeg, the harpooner. He meets Ishmael at the hostel, in comical circumstances and the two men become friends; more than that, they are joined by a "marriage" which forces them to look out for each other. They then board the same ship and finally, out of necessity, pursue the same goal.

During this initial experience, the hero is brought out of the world of the ordinary man, the known world, the comforting world, by boarding the *Pequod*, to discover a new world, which here is the world of the whalers. He hunts cetaceans for hours or entire days, to kill them and collect the fruits (oil, flesh, skin, spermaceti). While exploring this unknown universe, the hero faces many difficulties: storms and typhoons at sea, which severely test the sailors' determination; entire days spent lying in wait for a whale blow; the loss of friends. The hero also comes close to death: at the end of chapter 48, as the whalers are following a group of toothed whales in the fog, Ishmael's boat is hit by one of the whales and all the sailors on board are thrown into the sea. Pulled out by the *Pequod*, the hero was close to death.

Learning is another important step in his journey. The hero has to take something from this experience, he has to have developed when he returns from his journey by witnessing what he has been through. What Ishmael, and through him, the reader, is going to take from this journey, this hunt for whales and for *the* whale, is that natural powers are always superior to man, who cannot have complete control over life's events. We come back to the novel's symbolism: there is a superior power, a universal God, who presides over everybody's destiny. Opposing this destiny, such as Ahab before drowning, is a lost cause. This is the lesson that Ishmael must take from the adventure and, saved by higher powers, like a new prophet, transformed in his soul but unchanged in body, he returns to the ordinary world to tell them about his experience.

AHAB, THE OTHER ODYSSEUS

In Ancient Greek, Odysseus means "the angry". Isn't Ahab also an angry man, driven by his desire for vengeance on the sea monster? The comparison between the two heroes is of course simplistic, but absolutely justified.

Like Odysseus, the protagonist of the *Odyssey* (epic poem by Homer, Greek poet from the 8th century BC) who roams the seas searching for his homeland and in the hope of finding his wife Penelope, Ahab roams the seas in search of the object of his obsessional insanity since his last whaling trip: Moby Dick, the monstrous white whale who tore off his leg. For these two heroes, the journey consists of wandering, with an almost impossible goal, seeming to get further away each day.

Ahab's madness increasingly develops as the story brings him closer to the object of his quest: sometimes he stays pent-up in his cabin, muttering and scrutinising the maps in search of the best route to follow, sometimes, sitting on the ship's deck, he watches the sea as though it numbs him from the rage that devours him. His monologues and extortion of the sailors are signs of the madness that consumes him:

> "So full of his thought was Ahab, that at every uniform turn that he made, now at the main-mast and now at the binnacle, you could almost see that thought turn in him as he turned, and pace in him as he paced; so completely possessing him, indeed, that it all but seemed the inward mould of every outer movement.
> 'D'ye mark him, Flask?' whispered Stubb; 'the chick that's in him pecks the shell. 'Twill soon be out.'
> The hours wore on; - Ahab now shut up within his cabin; anon, pacing the deck, with the same intense bigotry of purpose in his aspect." (Chapter 36).

While Odysseus and Ahab are comparable in the planning of their journey and their wandering, they are also very different, not least in terms of their destiny, the end that is reserved for them in their respective stories. In fact, despite all of the temptations that present themselves to Odysseus during his adventure (the sirens or Circe the magician who wants to keep him there with her), the hero remains strong and dedicated to his ultimate goal: to find his country and get his wife back. He does not succumb to the journey's many attractions, to the illusions of happiness that he sees, and he returns to the real world. His numerous detours were not futile, but affirmed, even exacerbated, his desire to return.

This is completely contrary to Captain Ahab. He gets carried away by his madness, his fixed idea of finding the white whale who then would perhaps turn out to only be an illusion, a fantastical construction appearing in front of sailors that have been at sea for too long – and their doubt would be legitimate. Blinded by hate and fascination for this marine monster, he drowns, literally and figuratively. Contrary to the hero in the *Odyssey*, his journey was one-way and destined for death.

FURTHER REFLECTION

SOME QUESTIONS TO THINK ABOUT...

- Melville's novel is both symbolic and metaphysical. Prove this with some examples.
- Some chapters in the book are constructed like acts of theatre (stage directions, mentioning each character's name before he speaks). How does this particular structure change the reader's perception of the scene, compared with the story's other scenes?
- How does this adventure shape Ishmael's character and cause him to develop? What do we call these types of stories?
- In Moby-Dick, or The Whale, expectation is very important for many of the characters (Ishmael, Ahab, the crew members). Explain why.
- What do the many encyclopaedic digressions about whales and the hunting world bring to the story? Use extracts from the book in your answer.
- Moby-Dick, or The Whale is a reflection, a microcosm of American society during that era (the start of the 19th century). Explain this regarding the crew's organisation and this quotation taken from the book: "the native American liberally provides the brains, the rest of the world as generously supplying the muscles" (Chapter 27).
- In chapter 3 ("The Spouter-Inn"), Ishmael, seeing Queequeg for the first time, says "Ignorance is the parent of fear". Comment on this phrase by examining the development of Ishmael and Queequeg's relationship. How could we also apply this quotation to the many chapters

of chapters of cetology that are interspersed in the novel?

- At the end of the epilogue, when Ishamel sees the Rachel approaching as it is coming to rescue him, is, on the whole, quite ironic. Explain this statement.
- Moby-Dick, or The Whale was inspired by the author's real life. Explain this fact by researching the elements that may have influenced him.
- Moby-Dick, or The Whale has inspired many adaptations itself. Compare John Huston's film (1956) to the original novel.

We want to hear from you!
Leave a comment on your online library
and share your favourite books on social media!

FURTHER READING

REFERENCE EDITION

- Melville, H. (1983) *Moby-Dick, or The Whale*. California: University of California Press.

REFERENCE STUDIES

- Abensour, C. and Goeury, M. (2004) *La littérature nord-américaine*. Paris: Pocket.
- Expositions (2016) A la recherche de Moby Dick. Dossier pédagogique. *Bibliothèque national de France*. [Online]. [Accessed 9 September 2016]. Available from: <http://expositions.bnf.fr/lamer/pedago/moby/index.htm>
- Bleton, T. (2016) *Moby Dick:* La rumeur en voyage. *Zone critique*. [Online]. [Accessed 14 August 2015]. Available from: <http://zone-critique.com/2015/08/14/moby-dick-herman-melville/>
- Herman Melville "Moby Dick". *Revue Indications*.
- Niemeyer, M. (2006) *Moby Dick*, un classique américan. *Le magazine littéraire*. [Online]. [Accessed 9 September 2016]. Available from: <http://www.magazine-litteraire.com/mensuel/456/moby-dick-classique-ameri-cain-01-09-2006-21971> p. 36
- Richir, M. (1996) Melville. Les assises du monde. Paris: Hachette Livre.
- Sachs, V. (1970) Le mythe de l'Amerérique et Moby Dick de Melville. Annales. Économies, Sociétés, Civilisations. [Online]. [Accessed 9 September 2016]. Available from: <http://www.persee.fr/doc/ahess_0395-2649_1970_

num_25_6_422299> p. 1547-1565.

ADAPTATIONS

Amongst many adaptations of Melville's work, it is worth noting:

- *Moby Dick.* (1956) [Film]. John Huston. Dir. USA: Moulin Productions Inc.
- *Moby Dick.* (1998) [Television miniseries]. Francis Ford Coppola. Dir. Australia: Nine Network Australia.
- *In the Heart of the Sea.* (2015) [Film]. Ron Howard. Dir. USA: Warner Bros.

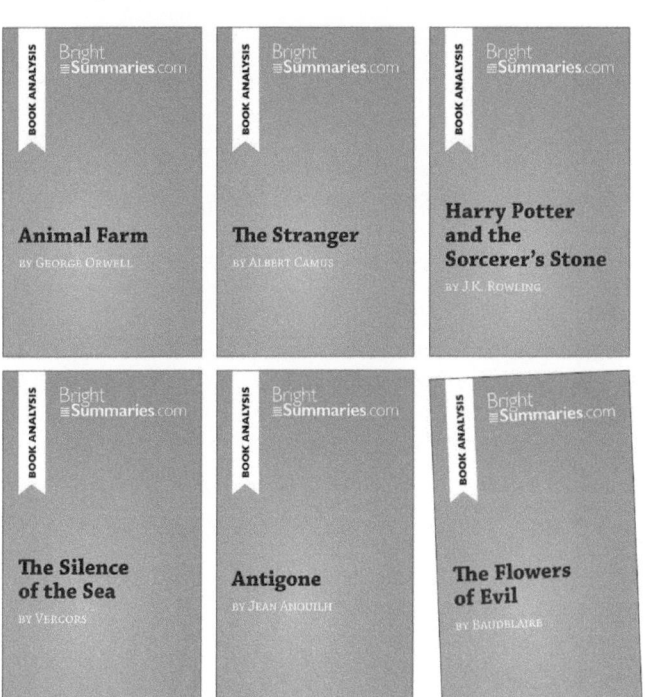

www.brightsummaries.com

Ebook EAN: 9782806279651

Paperback EAN: 9782806284440

Legal Deposit: D/2016/12603/391

Cover: © Primento

Digital conception by Primento, the digital partner of publishers.